Pet Care

Hamsters

Rebecca Sjonger & Bobbie Kalman

Photographs by Marc Crabtree

Crabtree Publishing Company

www.crabtreebooks.com

Hamsters

A Bobbie Kalman Book

Dedicated by Rebecca Sjonger
To Gepke Sjonger and Emma Hardie, both "great" grandmas!

Editor-in-Chief
Bobbie Kalman

Writing team
Rebecca Sjonger
Bobbie Kalman

Substantive editor
Kathryn Smithyman

Editors
Amanda Bishop
Kelley MacAulay

Art director
Robert MacGregor

Design
Margaret Amy Reiach

Production coordinator
Heather Fitzpatrick

Photo research
Crystal Foxton
Kristina Lundblad

Consultant
Dr. Michael A. Dutton, DVM, DABVP
Exotic and Bird Clinic of New Hampshire
www.exoticandbirdclinic.com

Special thanks to
Devan Cruickshanks and Scooter, Brody Cruickshanks,
Heather and Tim Cruickshanks, Steve Cruickshanks,
Kyle Foxton, Doug Foxton, Aimee Lefebvre, Alissa Lefebvre,
Jacquie Lefebvre, Jeremy Payne, Dave Payne, Kathy Middleton,
Natasha Barrett, Mike Cipryk and PETLAND

Photographs
Marc Crabtree: back cover, title page, pages 3, 4, 5, 6, 11, 12, 13, 14,
15, 16-17, 18 (top), 19 (top), 20, 21 (top), 22, 23, 24, 25, 28, 30, 31
Robert MacGregor: page 21 (bottom)
Other images by Comstock, Digital Stock and PhotoDisc

Illustrations
All illustrations by Margaret Amy Reiach

Digital prepress
Embassy Graphics

Printer
Worzalla Publishing Company

Crabtree Publishing Company

www.crabtreebooks.com   1-800-387-7650

PMB 16A	612 Welland Avenue	73 Lime Walk
350 Fifth Avenue	St. Catharines	Headington
Suite 3308	Ontario	Oxford
New York, NY	Canada	OX3 7AD
10118	L2M 5V6	United Kingdom

Cataloging-in-Publication Data
Sjonger, Rebecca.
  Hamsters / Rebecca Sjonger & Bobbie Kalman;
photographs by Marc Crabtree.
     p. cm. -- (Pet care series)
  Includes index.
  ISBN 0-7787-1753-4 (RLB) -- ISBN 0-7787-1785-2 (pbk.)
  1. Hamsters as pets--Juvenile literature. [1. Hamsters. 2. Pets.]
I. Kalman, Bobbie. II. Crabtree, Marc, ill. III. Title. IV. Series.
  SF459.H3S56 2004
  636.935'6--dc22
                                                    2003027237
                                                    LC

Contents

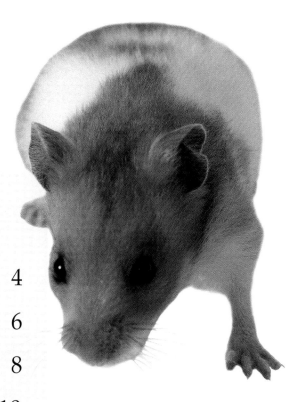

What are hamsters?

Hamsters are **mammals**. Mammals have fur or hair on their bodies. They also have backbones. Mother mammals make milk inside their bodies to feed their babies. Hamsters are part of a group of mammals called **rodents**. Most rodents are very small and have sharp front teeth.

A hamster's body

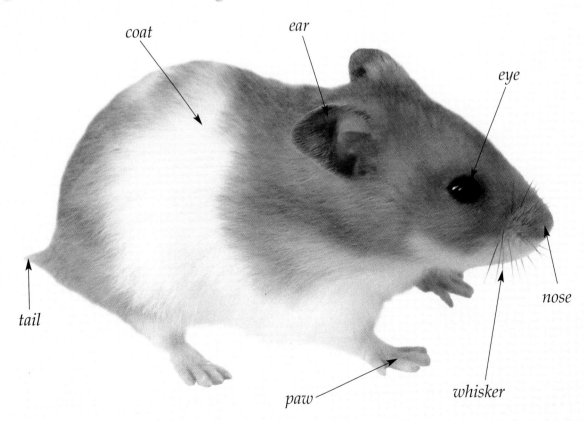

coat

ear

eye

tail

paw

whisker

nose

Hamster history

Pet hamsters are related to **wild hamsters**. Wild hamsters are not tame. They live in deserts and rocky areas. They dig underground **burrows**, or tunnels. Wild hamsters sleep in their burrows during the day to stay out of the hot sun. They gather food at night when it is cool and dark. Like wild hamsters, pet hamsters are active mainly at night. Most pet hamsters sleep all day long.

Pet hamsters love tunnels, tubes, and toys they can use as burrows.

The right pet for you?

Hamsters are cute and fun to watch as they scamper around their cages. They are small, so they do not need as much space as some other pets need. Hamsters sleep for most of the day. Waking a hamster to play with you during the day can upset it. If you wait until after dark to play with your hamster, it will be full of energy!

Would you take good care of a hamster?

Are you ready?

The questions below will help you and your family decide if you are ready for a hamster.

🐾 Do you have other pets that may scare or hurt a hamster?

🐾 Is there a quiet area in your home where you can put a cage?

🐾 Will you clean the entire cage at least once a week?

🐾 Who will feed the hamster and give it fresh water every day?

🐾 Do you have time to play with a hamster every evening?

🐾 Is anyone in your family **allergic** to hamsters?

All kinds of hamsters!

There are many **breeds**, or kinds, of hamsters living in the wild, but only a few hamster breeds are kept as pets. Syrian hamsters, Djungarian hamsters, Siberian hamsters, Chinese hamsters, and Roborovski hamsters are the breeds you will likely find in pet stores. Each kind of hamster looks and acts differently. Choose the breed you like the best!

Syrian hamsters are the largest pet hamsters. Their bodies are six to seven inches (15-18 cm) long.

Golden pets

Most pet hamsters are Syrian hamsters. They are also called golden hamsters because many have gold-colored fur. There are different types of Syrian hamsters, such as spotted gold Syrians or banded Syrians. The coat of each type differs in color, pattern, and length.

Djungarian hamsters are also called Russian hamsters. They have very short tails that may be hard to see.

Siberian hamsters are also known as winter white hamsters. They turn from grayish brown to white in the winter months.

Roborovski hamsters are the smallest pet hamsters. They grow to be around three inches (7.6 cm) long.

Chinese hamsters have slim bodies and inch-long (2.5 cm) tails.

Baby hamsters

Baby hamsters are called **puppies**. Up to fourteen puppies may be born at the same time in a **litter**, or group. When they are born, puppies are pink because they have not yet grown fur. They cannot see or hear. A mother hamster protects and feeds her puppies when they are very young. She snuggles beside them to keep them warm.

Puppy love

Puppies are very cute and fun to watch as they grow. However, if you let your hamster **mate** and have its own puppies, you will have a lot of animals to care for! You must find good homes for the puppies before they grow up. Keep male and female hamsters apart to stop unwanted puppies from being born.

Growing up

Puppies can see and hear ten days after they are born. Their fur grows soft and fluffy on their bodies. When puppies are three weeks old, they must leave their mothers. Most mother hamsters begin fighting with their puppies if they stay with her too long. The puppies may also begin to fight with one another if they are kept together after six weeks.

Male and female puppies can mate and make babies when they are about five weeks old.

Choosing your hamster

There are a few places where you can find a pet hamster. Check if your local **animal shelter** or your friends are giving away young hamsters for free. You can also buy a hamster from a **breeder** or a pet store. Make sure you get your pet from someone who takes very good care of animals!

A Syrian hamster is happiest when it can have a house to itself!

Three's a crowd

Syrian hamsters like living alone. If you put two or more Syrian hamsters together, they will fight and may hurt each other. Most other popular hamster breeds like to live in pairs. Choose two hamsters that are both males or both females and are from the same litter. They will play together and enjoy each other's company.

What to look for

Take your time when you are choosing the hamster you want to bring home with you. Some of the ways you can tell if it is healthy are listed below.

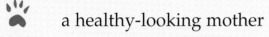 a healthy-looking mother

clean, smooth fur

a clean nose and bottom

bright, clear eyes that are not runny

easy, quiet breathing

no scratches or sores on its skin

active, curious behavior in the evenings

Getting ready

Before you bring your hamster home, get everything you need to care for it properly. These pages show what you will need.

Buy a large, comfortable cage.

Line the bottom of the cage with **bedding** *such as aspen shavings.*

Hamsters with long fur need to be brushed with a small **wire brush** *or a clean toothbrush.*

A small box or house gives your hamster a dark, quiet place to rest.

Buy a **ceramic** food bowl. Your hamster will not be able to tip it over or gnaw through it!

A **salt lick** helps your hamster get the salt it needs in its diet.

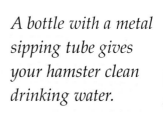

A bottle with a metal sipping tube gives your hamster clean drinking water.

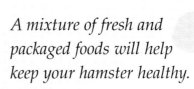

A mixture of fresh and packaged foods will help keep your hamster healthy.

Your hamster will love gnawing on fruit-tree branches!

Toys will keep your hamster from becoming bored. Toys will also give it exercise!

Welcome home!

When you pick up your new hamster, put it into a small cage or a cardboard box with air holes. Visit a **veterinarian** or "vet" on the way home. Your vet will check your hamster for any illnesses. When you arrive at home, give your hamster all the time it needs to get used to you and your family.

Happy hamster home

You can buy a cage at a pet store. Many cages have plastic bases with wire mesh tops. Make sure the spaces between all the wires are much smaller than the hamster is, or it may escape from the cage! It may also escape by eating through the plastic base, so the wires should go all the way down to the bottom of the cage.

sleeping house

Different levels give your hamster more space to play.

Tunnels must be roomy and have air holes.

The perfect place

Some of the things to look for when picking the best spot to put your hamster's cage are listed below.

🐾   quiet during the daytime

🐾   near a sunny window

🐾   temperature between 65°F and 80°F (18°C to 26°C)

🐾   not overly **humid**

Putting the water bottle outside of the cage saves space inside for your hamster!

salt lick

food bowl

Cover the floor of the cage with at least one inch (2.5 cm) of bedding. Avoid cedar and pine shavings—these woods could make your pet very sick!

Healthy hamster food

Hamsters need certain foods to stay healthy. You can buy food made just for hamsters at a pet store. This food is a mix of seeds, nuts, and dried plants. Clean and then fill your hamster's food bowl every evening. Hamsters also love eating fresh fruit and vegetables. You can give a small handful of chopped carrots, cucumbers, celery, grapes, strawberries, or apples to your hamster every day.

Your hamster stores food in its cheek pouches. It carries the food to hiding places around the cage!

Fresh water

Your hamster needs plenty of water to stay healthy. Make sure the bottle is always full of fresh water. Watch out for leaky bottles! Clean the water bottle every day.

Not for dinner!

Be very careful not to give your hamster any food that will make it sick!

- Fruits and vegetables that have not been rinsed properly may have harmful **pesticides** on them.

- **Citrus fruits**, such as oranges or grapefruits, are not healthy for your hamster.

- Never give your hamster rotten food! Make sure to take old food out of the cage every day.

- Candy and sugary treats will make your hamster ill.

- Eating **dairy foods**, such as milk or ice cream, can make your hamster sick.

Handsome hamsters

Your hamster will spend a lot of time **grooming**, or cleaning, itself. It uses its paws, tongue, and teeth to keep its body clean. Your pet may still need your help to look and feel its best, though!

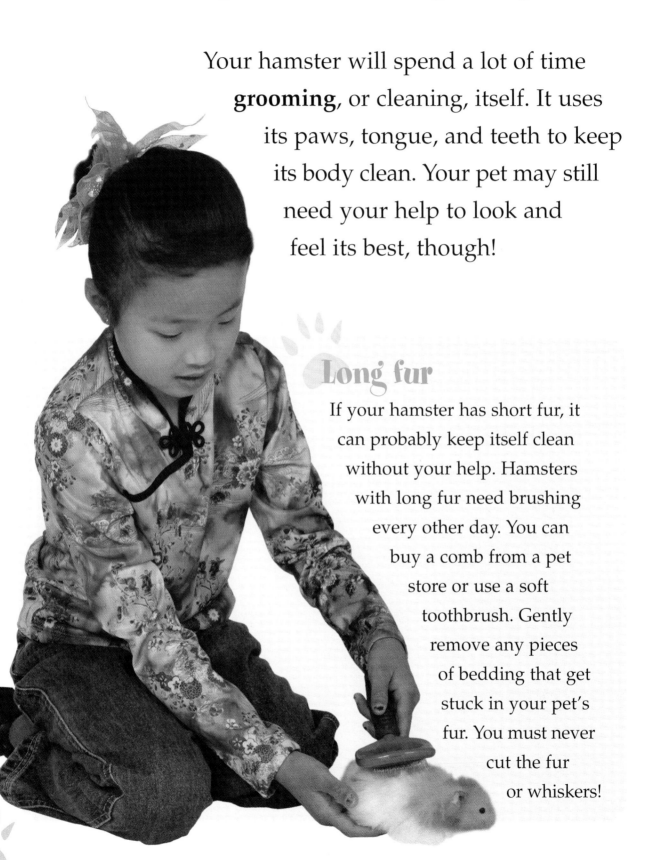

Long fur

If your hamster has short fur, it can probably keep itself clean without your help. Hamsters with long fur need brushing every other day. You can buy a comb from a pet store or use a soft toothbrush. Gently remove any pieces of bedding that get stuck in your pet's fur. You must never cut the fur or whiskers!

Terrific teeth

Hamsters have four **incisors**, or sharp front teeth, which never stop growing. You can help your hamster keep its teeth in good condition by giving it hard pieces of fruit-tree wood to gnaw on. Gnawing grinds down the teeth and keeps them from getting too long.

Clicky claws

If your hamster's claws grow so long that they begin to curl, ask your veterinarian to show you how to trim them. You must be very careful! If the claws are cut too short they may bleed. Put cardboard or wood into your hamster's cage for scratching. Scratching will help prevent its claws from growing too long.

Always use clippers or scissors that are made just for trimming rodent claws.

Handle with care

After your hamster has had a day or two to explore its cage and become comfortable, you can begin training it to be **handled**, or picked up. Always wash your hands before and after handling your hamster.

Hands up!

At first, just let your hamster sniff your fingers and hands. It needs to become used to your smell. You can also offer it some leafy greens or other treats. Your hamster will come to your hand if it thinks that it will get some food!

Handy hamsters

After a few days of letting your hamster grow used to you, it may climb into your hand. Keep your hand flat against the floor. Let your hamster crawl from one hand to the other so it can keep moving around. You can now try picking up your hamster!

Use both hands when you pick up your hamster. Never pick it up by its arms, legs, or head!

Play time!

During their evening play time, hamsters are active and curious. They love running around, climbing, digging, and hiding. If there are not enough things for your hamster to do in its cage, it may become bored and unhappy. These pages show some hamster toys that you may want to include in your hamster's home.

Toys you can change around will double your hamster's fun!

24

Mixing it up

Try adding new toys or moving toys from one area of the cage to another area. These changes will keep your pet interested in its cage! Never change more than one thing at a time. Your hamster may become confused if too much changes in its home.

Save cardboard tubes to make playthings for your hamster.

An exercise wheel is a great place for your hamster to burn off energy!

Sending messages

Your hamster can send messages to people and other animals without making a sound. Watch how your hamster moves its body. It may be trying to tell you something! Sometimes you will know how your hamster feels because of noises it makes. The common ways that hamsters express themselves are on these pages.

A big stretch and a yawn mean that a hamster is content.

A hamster that is crawling along the ground looking for a hiding place may be scared.

A hamster standing on its back legs with its nose in the air is very curious.

If a hamster is ready to fight, it may lie on its back with its paws up in the air.

Listen up!

Hamsters cannot speak, but they can make sounds that help you understand them. If your hamster squeaks, watch out! Hamsters often squeak before they bite. They may also growl or hiss if they are threatened. Pay close attention if your hamster begins to squeal. Squealing can mean that your hamster is scared or in pain.

Staying safe

If hamsters are not handled carefully or are disturbed while they are sleeping, they may nip or bite. Remember that hamsters have sharp teeth! You can avoid being bitten by your hamster if you leave it alone when it is sleeping. Never startle it when you pick it up! Move slowly and always handle your hamster gently.

Show your family and friends how to handle your hamster properly. If there are a lot of unfamiliar people playing with your hamster, it may become nervous.

Stay indoors

Letting your hamster go outdoors is a bad idea. A hamster moves very fast! It will likely run for a hiding place. Your hamster will be in trouble if a cat or a bird finds it before you do.

Free to roam

Before you let your hamster run freely in a room, look for these possible dangers.

- Are there doors or windows that your hamster may use to escape?

- Are there any areas or items in which your hamster may hide?

- Is there anything in the room that your hamster may damage with its teeth or claws?

- Are there **poisonous** plants that your hamster can reach and eat?

- Are there exposed electrical cords that may harm your hamster if it bites them?

Pets such as dogs may be a great danger to your hamster!

Visiting a vet

A veterinarian is a medical doctor who treats animals. He or she will help you keep your hamster healthy. If you think that your hamster may be sick, take it to see a vet right away. The sooner your hamster is treated by a vet, the better its chances are of surviving an illness!

If you ever have any questions about your hamster's health, your vet can help you.

When to get help

It is very important to take your hamster to a vet at the first signs of an illness. Watch for the warning signs listed below.

- sleeping more than usual
- eating less food than the hamster usually eats
- runny eyes or nose
- sores or scabs on its skin
- losing fur or having a dull coat
- heavy, loud breathing
- a wet bottom

Best friends

Caring for your hamster means spending time with it every day. You need to feed it, groom it, and play with it. Happy, healthy hamsters live for two to three years. Enjoy all the time you have with your hamster!

Words to know

Note: Boldfaced words that are defined in the book may not appear on this page.

allergic Describing someone who has a physical reaction to something

animal shelter A center that cares for animals that do not have owners

breeder A person who brings hamsters together so the hamsters can make babies

ceramic Describing something that is made out of baked clay

citrus fruit Juicy fruit that has a thick skin, such as an orange

dairy food Food made with milk and milk products

humid Describing air that contains water vapor, which makes the air damp or moist

mate To join two animals together to make babies

pesticide Chemical made to kill insects

poisonous Describing something that has substances in it that may harm or kill an animal

veterinarian A medical doctor who treats animals

Index

1 2 3 4 5 6 7 8 9 0 Printed in the U.S.A. 3 2 1 0 9 8 7 6 5 4